A Little Treat

Frank Murdocco

methuen | drama
LONDON • NEW YORK • OXFORD • NEW DELHI • SYDNEY

METHUEN DRAMA
Bloomsbury Publishing Plc, 50 Bedford Square, London, WC1B 3DP, UK
Bloomsbury Publishing Inc, 1359 Broadway, New York, NY 10018, USA
Bloomsbury Publishing Ireland, 29 Earlsfort Terrace, Dublin 2,
D02 AY28, Ireland

BLOOMSBURY, METHUEN DRAMA and the Methuen
Drama logo are trademarks of Bloomsbury Publishing Plc.

First published in Great Britain 2025

Copyright © Frank Murdocco, 2025

Frank Murdocco has asserted their right under the Copyright, Designs
and Patents Act, 1988, to be identified as Author of this work.

For legal purposes the Acknowledgments on p. iv
constitute an extension of this copyright page.

Photography by Mod Schwalbe

All rights reserved. No part of this publication may be: i) reproduced or
transmitted in any form, electronic or mechanical, including photocopying,
recording or by means of any information storage or retrieval system without
prior permission in writing from the publishers; or ii) used or reproduced in
any way for the training, development or operation of artificial intelligence (AI)
technologies, including generative AI technologies. The rights holders
expressly reserve this publication from the text and data mining exception as
per Article 4(3) of the Digital Single Market Directive (EU) 2019/790.

Bloomsbury Publishing Plc does not have any control over, or responsibility
for, any third-party websites referred to or in this book. All internet addresses
given in this book were correct at the time of going to press. The author and
publisher regret any inconvenience caused if addresses have changed or sites
have ceased to exist, but can accept no responsibility for any such changes.

No rights in incidental music or songs contained in the work are hereby
granted and performance rights for any performance/presentation
whatsoever must be obtained from the respective copyright owners.

All rights whatsoever in this play are strictly reserved and application
for performance etc. should be made before rehearsals begin to the author
via Bloomsbury Publishing, performance.permissions@bloomsbury.com.

No performance may be given unless a licence has been obtained.

A catalogue record for this book is available from the British Library.

Library of Congress Control Number: 2025945581

ISBN: PB: 978-1-3505-9345-9
ePDF: 978-1-3505-9348-0
eBook: 978-1-3505-9347-3

Series: Modern Plays

Typeset by Mark Heslington Ltd, Scarborough, North Yorkshire
Printed and bound in Great Britain

For product safety related questions contact
productsafety@bloomsbury.com.

To find out more about our authors and books visit
www.bloomsbury.com and sign up for our newsletters.

For my parents.
For everything.

Acknowledgments

So many people have made this play happen in so many ways and I cannot begin to express my gratitude to them. I'm going to try to, anyway.

Thank you to my brothers, Jonathan and Christian, along with Maria and Isabel, Jonathan, Delilah, and Sophia, for your constant, unending support and love.

My amazing aunts and uncles, Aunt Catherine and Uncle Richard, Aunt Kathy and Uncle Dennis, Uncle John and Aunt Debbi, and Aunt Gerri. My incredible cousins, nieces, and nephews. The Godwins. All the beautiful family and friends who all fill both categories effortlessly. Thank you all for your never-ending love and support.

Steph Miller – thank you so much for the boundless collaboration and support you have given me and this play.

To the team at Junto for bringing this show to life.

To the Bloomsbury and Methuen team for bringing it to shelves.

This play is dedicated to my parents, but a dedication will never be enough of a thank you – nothing will. Your constant support, infinite love, and tireless dedication is the greatest gift anyone could ever receive. Thank you.

And Christopher, who has made so much possible in so many ways. You and Basil are my world. Ours is my favorite team. I'll never know what I did to deserve you, but it's probably best I don't question it. I love you.

A Little Treat had its world premiere in August of 2024 at the 2024 Edinburgh Fringe Festival at Greenside at George's Street, Mint Studio Theatre.

It had its New York Premiere in September of 2025 at the East Village Basement.

The role of Greg was performed by Frank Murdocco.

Both productions were directed by Steph Miller.

The productions were presented and produced by Junto Entertainment.

For information on accessing the rights to perform *A Little Treat*, please visit www.frankmurdocco.com/writing

Characters

Gregory Hurst, *et al. – 29ish – (he/him) kind, optimistic, aimless, anxious, hopeful, beaten down, energized. A creative, though he's not sure what that means (or what that looks like), Greg moved to New York City for college from Connecticut. He's stayed put since. This is his story through his eyes.*

The character of Gregory is male presenting, but may be played by any performer of any gender, identity, race, etc.

Setting

Inwood, March 2020, and onward, across New York City.

Notes on the Set

The projections mentioned throughout the script, along with sound and lighting, are more suggestions than anything else. All scenic elements shouldn't be too literal – everything can feel abstract and through the prism of Greg's mind.

Notes on Performance

The audience should serve as the second performer in the play – when Greg speaks, it is direct address to the audience.

Anytime Greg says something in quotes, he is speaking to another character within the story.

Every other character is presented through the lens of Greg but fully embodied as a whole being. When they speak, Greg disappears. The performer is to fully embody that character and then return to Greg's form once the other character is finished.

The performer does not leave the chair for nearly the entirety of the play, until the stage directions say to do so.

About the Author

Frank Murdocco is a New York-based writer and performer. He made his New York stage debut with his first solo show, *The Public and Private Deaths of Carol O'Grady* at the 2018 New York International Fringe Festival. The production then transferred off-Broadway to HERE Arts Center's main stage. Since his stage debut, Murdocco has actively performed off-Broadway, in television and film, and has provided voiceover for countless commercial campaigns.

As a writer, he has held residencies with Gingold Theatrical Group, Arthouse Productions, the Cold Read Series, and the Artist Co-Op. His plays include *I Didn't Mean to Scream So Loud*, *I Want the World (And When I Get It, I'll Want Something Else)*, *Legume*, *O'Grady*, and *A Little Treat*.

A graduate of Stony Brook University, Murdocco was the recipient of the Chair's Award for Outstanding Achievements as a Theatre Practitioner.

He is a proud member of the Actors' Equity Association and the Dramatists Guild.

@frankmurdocco, www.frankmurdocco.com

Author's Note

I wrote this play about a single character in a universal time. The first draft was completed in 2023. When I finished it, I wondered if we'd still be feeling the fallout from that time.

In 2024, when I first performed it, we were. It is now 2025 and we still are.

We've lost so much and we're all still trying to figure out what we've gained.

In a small way, that's what this play is about.

Content warning: Mental health, discrimination, references to suicide.

A Little Treat

LIGHTS UP ON:

A single stool sits in the center of a stage.

The stool is illuminated by a single light.

Rapidly, the lights cut to black.

They come back up to find **Greg**, *29 and a half, sitting on the stool.*

He is about to sneeze.

Greg I –

I'm gonna sneeze

He goes to – he cannot.

One second

He goes to sneeze again. Nothing.

It's at, it's like at the tip of my nose

He tries again. Still nothing.

It's not coming.

God I hate that feeling

Also, I was going to cover my mouth I think it looked like I wasn't going to cover my mouth, but I was.

I wasn't free balling the sneeze, I just wasn't at the covering my mouth point yet.

I say that because we just met and I don't want your first impression of me to be that I'm the kind of person who doesn't cover his mouth when he sneezes.

Those people are the reason we're all *here*, when you think about it. I mean, there's *a lot* of reasons why we're here but showering people with your spittle certainly didn't help the cause.

And if we're here for me to share my experience – which, presumably is why we are here – I don't want you thinking that there is an undertone of recklessness running beneath all of this, because there isn't. And, you know, for the longest time I had no interest in sharing this experience, even thinking about it.

But I get this new therapist, I have this therapist, she's very nice, she's a very nice dresser, which I love, I love a nice dresser.

She wears pantsuits, but not in this Hillary Clinton way, hers have this nice silhouette.

Not that there's anything wrong with a Hillary Clinton pantsuit, I loved her pantsuits. Not in an idealistic way. I'm not one of those – I mean, I obviously voted for her, but I'm not – I've never like venerated her. I'm not saying I dislike Hillary Clinton, I love Hillary Clinton.

My therapist, though, she – she said that I should feel comfortable telling my story, that in order to let go of it I first must share it. Which –

I'm sorry, I just want to go back to the Hillary Clinton thing. When I said I love Hillary Clinton, I didn't mean I *love* Hillary Clinton. I meant, I admire her, I guess. Or – no, admiration feels right. Does it? I have no clue what I'm saying.

I'm sorry, I'm nervous. And when I'm nervous I overshare. I overshare when I'm not nervous, too, but when I'm nervous, I'm like. You can't stop me. I can't be stopped.

He looks at the stool.

I'm also incredibly uncomfortable, right now. Like physically. I have these hemorrhoids, and when I'm sitting like this, it's really uncomfortable. They're like butted up right against the wood – you really do not need to know that, you don't even know my name

My name is Greg by the way. Just Greg. Not Gregory, I hate Gregory.

So, my name's Greg and – what was I saying?

I was talking about sneezing, and my therapist, and –

(*Filling the stage is a projection which reads MARCH 11TH, 2020, accompanied by a loud bang.*)

RIGHT, okay. So, so, so this is where we're going to start, if that works for you – I'm going to assume that works for you.

March 11th, 2020.

I'm home, in my tiny apartment. I love my apartment, it's the most perfect 350 square feet at the upper tip of Manhattan. It's five minutes from the park, and if you look out in just the right direction, you see the sun hitting the trees and bouncing off all the other buildings and it's like the city is completely mine.

It's around 12 p.m. and I'm getting ready to go to work – I work as a cycling, singing tour guide in New York City.

I lead bike tours and sing in between facts about Central Park.

It's more of a karaoke situation. It's fun, it might not sound fun, but it's fun, I promise.

On March 11th, 2020 I was getting ready to head down to work when my phone rings. It's my manager, Kenneth, on the other line.

A phone rings.

'Hi Kenneth' I say

Kenneth Gregory

Greg I *loathe* being called Gregory. And Kenneth always makes the active choice to call me Gregory, despite possessing the knowledge that I do not like being called Gregory.

Can I say something mean? Kenneth is – he's. He's a nasty twink. Really, he just has a putrid presence.

Kenneth Gregory?

Gregory 'Morning, Kenneth' I say

Kenneth It's the afternoon. Anyway, Gregory, I just got off the phone with Phyllis –

Greg Phyllis owns the company with her husband.

'What did she have to say' I ask. Occasionally, Ken will give me notes on my performance – which is *insane* considering he isn't on the tours with me.

Kenneth Well, we are growing concerned about this virus out there

Greg 'Right' I say to him. I don't want to fess up that really I wasn't aware there was a virus out there. That I only knew of it in the periphery. The same way you sort of look at a bad day on the stock market, think *well that's bad for the people that affects, but I'm not one of those people.*

Kenneth continues

Kenneth Well, Phyllis believes we should suspend tours at this time and I agree. Your health and safety is of the utmost importance to us.

Greg 'Right' I say. The funny thing about Kenneth's authority complex is he makes $3 more than me an hour. So, it's like, calm down pal. That's when I realize – money.

I was doing three tours today. That's like $100 in tips, plus $50 a tour.

'Wait' I say –

Kenneth You will be paid for the first two tours, don't worry

Greg 'Okay, but what about the third' I ask

Kenneth What about it?

Greg 'I'm booked for three tours today'

Kenneth Right

Greg 'Right?'

Kenneth Right.

Greg 'So . . .' I say

Kenneth Well, Phyllis only gave me clearance to pay for the first two, not the third

Greg 'But I'm missing three tours' I say

Kenneth Yes, no, I got that bit Gregory, but none of our guests will be paying for any of the tours

Greg 'Right' I say, 'but that's not my issue'

Kenneth Okay, tone

Greg 'I'm not taking a tone, I'm just –'

Kenneth What I can offer is what I can offer. That said, I understand your frustration and will pass your concerns along to Phyllis. Be well.

Greg 'Wait so when will I start doing tours again?'

Kenneth Oh.

Well . . . I don't know

Greg 'A day? Few days?'

Kenneth I think a little longer than that, maybe, I don't know, two weeks – do you know what's going on right now?

Greg 'Of course I do' I say

Kenneth What's your grocery situation like?

Greg 'What?' I ask

Kenneth Your groceries? How stocked up are you? I'm seeing online that people are stockpiling.

Greg 'Stockpiling, how' I ask.

Kenneth You should really run to a grocery store and get food for the next week or so. I'm doing the same.

Greg I'm taken by this small show of concern.

Does Kenneth . . . care about me?

'Thank you, Kenneth' I say

Kenneth Sure, Gregory

Greg And he hangs up.

What an odd, odd moment. I make a mental note to consider not hating Kenneth, then prepare to go down to the nearest grocery store which is

The stage illuminates into a blurry supermarket, while the sounds of feral arguments play over **Greg**.

A SHIT SHOW

AN ABSOLUTE SHIT SHOW

I am positive the entirety of New York City has descended upon this store – all five boroughs, I'm including Staten Island

I have never seen a store so packed. And people so feral.

Someone reaches directly into my cart and takes one of my bottles of Everything But The Bagel Seasoning

There is shouting, there is pulling, there is pushing, there is a man in an incredibly tight bike suit and I can see the full outline of his penis – that one's kind of normal for New York

At any rate – it is kill or be killed. And

At one point I find myself elbowing for a bag of frozen tilapia. I don't eat fish

I am swept up in a wave of insanity and have no clue what I just bought.

The store disappears and the sounds fade.

I get home, to my apartment, my little corner of the world. And I begin to unbag my groceries and I start to realize – I have no fucking clue what's going on

I thought Kenneth was just being dramatic

And now I'm looking at the pile of food that I bought and

I hardly got anything substantial. It's all candy and seasonings. And that bag of fish. And somehow I spent $120.

And I become overwhelmed and inside of my chest, a familiar rapid warmth starts to swell and radiate throughout my body, pulsing, and that's when my alarm goes off

A phone alarm rings.

It is 7 p.m.

And then

Everything starts to feel okay.

The alarm silences.

A glow fills the stage.

Greg *instantly decompresses.*

7 p.m.

My favorite time of day

7 p.m. is Little Treat Time.

Little Treat Time is my designated point in the day for myself and the small joys that populate my life.

Five-and-a-half years ago I was having a rough go of it.

The restaurant I was working at closed, this guy I was seeing turned out to be an asshole, he probably always was an asshole, but . . .

Then, then my old roommate had kicked me out – okay, she moved in with her boyfriend, but that's, it's a lot like kicking me out.

10 A Little Treat

And I had stopped talking to my dad, completely . . .

All in one month.

So, I made a decision for myself. Everyday, regardless of what was going on.

Every day at 7 p.m., I have a little treat.

Now,

The rules for what constitute a little treat are simple:

It must spark joy and that joy has to be immediate.

That's it.

Every day, my phone alarm goes off at 7 p.m. I shut out the world and give myself something fun. A pint of ice cream. My favorite show. Listening to an album by one of those women all gay men like.

Simple joys, simple pleasures, unmitigated, just for myself.

It's a small reminder to me that no matter what – I deserve something good.

At 7 p.m., I look around at the little world I've built for myself, and think about the bigger world it exists in and all of the bullshit that comes from there and I shut it out.

That, that is really the core of a little treat – shutting out the bullshit.

It is a dedication to the self to say *fuck the world, this hour is mine and mine alone*

As I begin to decide on what that day's little treat would be, my phone rings

His phone rings.

It's my mother

I let it ring for a second before I pick it up and hear

Ellen Oh Christ, Greg, I thought something happened

Greg 'Why would you think that?'

Ellen You took forever to answer.

Greg 'I just didn't hear it ringing' I say

Ellen Oh, oh, it's 7 p.m. Your little – your fun time. Should I call back?

Greg 'Don't call it that'

Ellen That's what it is, isn't it?

Greg 'When you say fun time, it sounds like there's something odd going on'

Ellen Well, what's your, your treat for the day

Greg 'There's a new Real Housewives I'm going to try out. And I got a pint of Haagen Dazs'

Ellen God, I wish I had your job. You just burn those calories off. If I had one spoonful of that ice cream, do you know what would happen? My fupa would pop my jeans open.

Greg 'Okay, Mom' I say

Ellen Do you know what FUPA stands for, Hannah taught me.

Anyway, I was calling because I wanted to see if you thought maybe you should come home?

Greg Come home?

'Why would I come home' I ask

Ellen I don't know, Greggy, I'm not sure how bad this is and you're all alone out there

Greg To be clear, my mom lives forty-five minutes away from me – less than, even. I'm from Connecticut, without traffic, she could get to me in half an hour

'Mom, I'm not coming home. I'm fine' I say

12 A Little Treat

Ellen Just think about it. Greg.

Please, for me.

Greg That, that gets me. Because she only ever says *please, for me* when she *really* wants something. And I'm not going home, I know I am not moving home because someone in god knows where has a cold. But, anytime my mom has said *Please, for me* I become racked with guilt.

The last time she said it was when I told her I was done speaking with my dad, and my mom was so annoyed at me for that, which I never understood because that whole relationship is so fractured, it's so.

Well, it's a long story –

Well, a medium sized story, actually,

It's – what am I doing, I'll just tell you it.

When I was seventeen, my dad was arrested for involvement in a Ponzi scheme.

Not for running a Ponzi scheme, but for being involved in it.

He was the right hand man to the right hand man of the guy behind all of it.

Basically, he helped someone *help someone* steal from people.

He was in charge of the set-up, getting people into his office to speak to his boss. And he was good at it, too.

He'd come to all these school events and a few days later my friends' rich parents were in his boss's office forking over millions of dollars to invest.

And it was bullshit. All bullshit.

They lost all of it.

Retirement funds, college funds, life savings. All of it just disappeared because of my dad.

Well not my dad, my dad's boss

Well my dad's boss's boss.

My dad was a low level player. That, that to me is the worst part of it. – I mean fuck, if you're gonna be a criminal, at least be *the* criminal. Being middle management? It's embarrassing.

So he gets out of jail just desperate for a relationship with me, but I was an adult, now. Not the type he envisioned, I guess. It was like, every room I was in with him, I felt so uncomfortable. Finally, I say I'm moving to the city and he says something along the lines of 'that's what all you gays do' and it wasn't a big thing, but it was *a* thing.

A thing in combination with a million things

So I said fuck this.

And I made the active choice to let go.

A beat.

That wasn't nearly as long a story as I thought it would be, was it?

Isn't it so funny, everything feels so big in your head but then when you start to describe it, it's so small in context.

After my mom tells me to come home, I start to worry. Which, if you didn't notice, comes naturally to me. So I put on Real Housewives to calm me down, which usually works, but tonight.

Nothing would help.

So I decide to text Hannah. My sister. She's a resident at Yale Med School.

Greg *and* **Hannah**'s *texts are projected. It's clear the conversation is mostly one sided, with messages from* **Hannah** *going unanswered.*

Hannah and I don't talk much because – well, I'll be honest, she makes me feel inadequate

It's not her fault, she doesn't intentionally do that, it's not like she taunts me with her success.

It's like – you know when you're going to a party and you're like I'm going to bake a cake, and someone else shows up to the party with this fucking incredible cake that they've made and you're standing there holding this little pathetic, frosted thing you worked on for hours and the host is like *oh, well thank you for making that* and then all anyone does is talk about the other cake that that other person made and your sad little pathetic baked good is sitting on the edge of the dessert table, while their cake sits at the center?

It's a lot like that only the cake is life and the host is my mother.

That night, I text Hannah

He pulls out his phone, begins to text her.

One sentence: *What the fuck is going on*

We see his text projected.

Almost instantly she responds: *It's bad*

The stage lights darken as the text stays illuminated.

The lights rise and the text disappears.

Later I can't sleep. *That's* when I go down the rabbit hole.

Headlines begin to fill the stage along with tweets, infographics, and comments.

I use my mom's cable login to watch Rachel Maddow. What a delightful lesbian. Really.

My phone reaches 3 percent as I tear through post after post, tweet after tweet trying to make heads and tails of all of it

And I can't. And I hate that, I am such a control freak

I love *control*

So, I step back and decide. In the uncertainty, I will do what I do best – find certainty.

We are supposed to stay inside, that's what everyone is saying. So that's what I do

I fuck around until

The phone alarm rings.

It's 7 p.m.

Each night, I weigh my options, assess what my treat will be, make my choice, and tumble into bliss.

A phone alarm is heard.

Some nights it's cookies and Real Housewives

The phone alarm rings.

Some nights it's stalking my high school bully. *He's gay now!*

It rings again.

Some nights it's spending $20 of my unemployment check on something stupid

It rings once more.

Some nights it's a combination of three, some nights it's even more.

And as I tear through more and more evenings of treats,

I begin to recognize something

I hate people and I love myself

I am my own best friend

Not only am I loving the isolation, I'm resenting its inevitable end.

Two weeks pass by in a flash. I run out of groceries and discover the magic of Instacart.

I don't have to leave my little apartment

A Little Treat

In a city of eight million, I cannot be annoyed by the other seven point nine nine.

Until

One day

The phone alarm rings.

It is 7 p.m.

And as I'm preparing a bowl of ice cream

I hear something

The light clamoring of pots and pans is heard, growing in noise.

It gets louder

And louder

And I open my window

The sound is insurmountable.

Greg *begins to shout over it.*

In a city of eight million, these other fuckers finally found a way to get to me

People are leaning over their fire escapes, banging pots and pans, cheering, screaming

The sound begins to fade out.

Around 7:02, the banging dissipates

I go to get my phone and realize it's been dead all day

I haven't looked at it, I've been on my laptop and napping every other hour

I plug it in, turn it on, and text my neighbor, Samuel. Sam is a seventy-six-year-old man who owns a flower shop in Midtown, he leaves me a fresh bouquet of flowers every week.

He can only be described as both glamorous and, well . . . what's a kind word for 'got some miles on him'?

His text is projected – 'What's all that noise?'

Within seconds, Sam calls me

Samuel (*a gravely, gravely voice with deep flirtation in it*)   Hi Greg

Greg   'How are you doing, Sam' I ask him

Samuel   Oh, terrible, just terrible.

This is awful

I hate it.

You know, I'm so used to seeing so many people at the shop, all of my regulars. I hate it.

I'm just staring at the wall, staring at the fucking wall.

It's making me nuts

And you must be going nuts, yourself. A nice young man like yourself, there must be so many places you want to be, so many people you want to see

Greg   'Yeah, yeah, no sure, it's, it's –'

Samuel   It's fucking awful, that's just what it is. Fucking awful. A nightmare, I tell you. Literally a nightmare.

I'm waking up in piles of sweat from it.

I have to keep doing laundry and I think the laundry is wearing my sheets down because I found a hole in one of the sheets the other day. And I wasn't the one who put it there!

Greg   'Right. Wait, what's that mean?'

Samuel   It's a wiener joke, Greg

Greg   'Oh, really? I – okay. Anyway, I texted you because –'

Samuel   Yeah, I know, I read that, what do you mean what's that noise?

Greg   He says

18 A Little Treat

I say 'You don't hear that clamoring, the pots and pans?'

Samuel Of course I do! I'm the one doing it, ya fool

Greg 'What for?' I ask

Samuel Greg, are you not watching the news?

Greg What's with everyone asking me that

'No, I am, I am. I haven't seen anything about it'

Samuel It's to thank the first responders

Greg 'What do you mean?' I ask

Samuel We've been doing it for like the last three days. At 7 p.m., we bang pots and pans for a minute to thank the doctors and the nurses and the firefighters and the ambulance men. I'm particularly thanking the firefighters

You're so silly. How'd you not hear all that noise?

Greg 'I'm not sure' I say, realizing the sound of belligerent middle aged women fighting on reality TV must drown anything else out

Samuel What are you doing down there anyway? I haven't seen you around

Greg 'Aren't we not supposed to go out?' I ask

Samuel Yeah, but, a little stroll for fresh air isn't bad. What are they calling it? Socially separate? No, um. Distanced. Socially Distanced

I started making those little masks for the building. I called you yesterday to see if you wanted one?

Greg 'You did?' I ask

Samuel Yesterday, and a few days before that

Greg 'You did?'

Samuel *No, baby, I'm talking out of my ass.* Of course I did, why would I make that up?

Greg 'Oh' I say. I now realize I hadn't used my phone in a *handful* of days. 7 p.m. had been hitting and I didn't even need my alarm. My intuition alone made me realize what time it is.

Samuel Greggy? You still there?

Greg 'Yeah' I say

Samuel Okay, well, I gotta go baby, I have a virtual poker night. Isn't that cute? My friend from the Y set up virtual poker nights and we all play this game online together, I'm so bad at it. But thank god I get to talk to someone. Call me tomorrow, I'm desperate to speak to someone. Or you could even slip up here to get your masks. We'll distance or whatever.

Greg 'Right, okay. I'll talk to you soon' I say

Samuel Don't be a stranger

Greg And he hangs up

And I realize I haven't spoken to my mother in four days

And I look down at my phone

To find fourteen missed calls from her

And eight from my sister

And about – *yeah*, ninety-three texts

I call my mom up and within seconds she –

Ellen GREGORY

Greg 'Hi' I say

Ellen Where the *fuck* have you been?

Greg 'What, I –'

Ellen I have been calling you for the last four-and-a-half days, waiting for a goddamn response from you. Your sister has been calling. We've been messaging you on Instagram, Facebook –

Greg 'I only use Twitter' I say

Ellen I KNOW. This morning, I made an account to discover you've been liking tweets about MasterChef all morning long. So I knew you were alive. Why don't you check your Twitter messages

Greg I check, and sure enough, there's one from my mom

Ellen Your goddamn Twitter likes were the only things that stopped me from calling hospitals – you know those are public, by the way?

Greg 'Wait, really?'

Ellen Where have you been – are you going out, are you seeing people? We're not allowed to do that, you know?

Greg 'Of course I'm not seeing anyone, I'm not nuts'

Ellen So where have you been?

Greg 'Home'

Ellen Home? HOME? You've been HOME?

Greg 'My phone's been dead'

Ellen For four-and-a-half days?

I thought a fucking drug addict broke into your apartment and sold your fingers for meth

Greg 'Ma, I'm sorry, really. I had no idea how much time had passed'

Ellen What do you mean you didn't know how much time had passed

Greg 'I just, I didn't know what day it was'

Ellen You had no idea four days have gone by? Have you been taking walks? Do you have masks? Of course you don't.

I have some I can give you. Maybe I can drive by your apartment?

Greg   I realize if I say no, I'll get another *please, for me* out of her so I say 'Sure, Mom, that would be nice'

Ellen   I won't get out of the car, but at least we could see each other. At this point, I want to do a proof of life on you

Greg   'Alright, Ma, calm down. It was four days'

And we hang up. And I look at my melted bowl of ice cream and clock how interrupted my little treat was. But the magic of little treat time is, I just make another.

Greg's *phone rings.*

The next morning, Samuel calls me

He picks up.

'Hi Sam'

Samuel   Look at that, he knows how to pick up a phone. I wanted to let you know, I made you a mask.

Greg   'Oh, thank you' I say

Samuel   I'm gonna leave it in front of your door, but I did want to let you know, there's a slight issue. I ran out of all my nice gingham and tartan prints. So the only one I had left was, well I figured you'll enjoy it anyway. But the mask came out a little phallic.

Greg   'Oh' I say

Samuel   I mean it's not actual cock and balls or anything like that, but it's. Well, it's eggplant emojis. I figured this'll work for a mask and you of all people would be the one to wear it

Greg   'Thank you?'

Sam drops the mask at my door and I decide to go outside for the first time since this began.

22 A Little Treat

Everything feels different

The sun is harsher, the wind feels sharper. And the penis mask is smothering my face.

The streets are completely empty. I cover about four blocks, someone's walking their dog – they wave at me while the dog takes a dump. I wave back. Which feels weird for New York. Towards the end of the block, there's this line of grocery trucks parked in the middle of the street, blocking traffic. But it doesn't matter, there's no cars coming or going.

I decide to walk home just in time for my mom to pull up in front of the building.

Ellen (*with fearful intensity*)   I'm gonna –

Greg   She shouts to me, pulling down a surgical mask

Ellen   I'm gonna step out of my car now, okay? Don't move, I'm gonna leave these bags here. They've got –

Greg   'Mom, you can stop shouting' I say, 'I can hear you'

Ellen (*shouting*)   One tub is chicken parm, another is eggplant parm, and another is just the parm. It's all rinds of Parmesan. Hannah taught me how to order the groceries but the only cheese they had was Parmesan so I got a ton of it. So I gave some to you.

Greg   'Ma, you don't have to shout'

Ellen   Okay, good. Don't come any closer, I'm getting out of my car

Greg   And she does, and I realize that she is wearing a poncho and gloves

'Why do you have that on' I ask

Ellen   I don't know, I just sort of – I didn't know what the city would be like

Greg   'Right' I say

Ellen I would ask my son who lives there, but he went into a fugue state for four days

Greg 'How's Hannah' I ask

Ellen She's living in the garage

Greg 'The garage?' I ask

Ellen You'd know these things if you kept up

Greg 'Why is she living in the garage, Ma?'

Ellen Because she's still working. She's working now more than ever. Some of the things she's seeing, Greg. It's awful. It's just awful. And she's so noble about it. You know, so 'Oh, it's just what I have to do. It's what I signed up for' but Greg, she is seeing things. People are dying in the line to the hospital. In the line.

Greg And the only thing I do with this information is feel some sort of immense guilt for being able to melt away for a week

Ellen Anyway

Greg My mom says, inching away from me in her protective gear

Ellen I'm going to start back, sweetheart, okay? Have you taken a walk?

Greg 'I just did' I tell her

Ellen Keep taking them

Greg She says

Ellen Because you need to get out, you look pale.

Greg 'I always look pale' I say

Ellen Right, well, you look paler.

Greg 'Wait, if you're going up Broadway, make sure to get onto 9th before 215, there's all these grocery trucks by the hospital'

Ellen Grocery trucks?

Greg 'Like delivery trucks'

Ellen Those aren't grocery trucks, Greg. Those are morgues.

Greg And my mom leaves

And I decide I'm going to discover some sort of rhythm.

Every morning I will go on one walk around the neighborhood

Every afternoon, I text my mom to tell her I am alive.

And every other day I call her

My 7 p.m. remains the same.

This pattern works for a little over a month, and I ease into May.

And my dad begins to call daily. Now, he's always called. But it used to be monthly, then it moved to weekly, and now. I have to give him points for persistence.

I know I could pick up. I know I could pick up and have some stunted conversation with him that's vaguely nauseating at best. But why bother myself with that?

That's when I discover that my sister has gotten back in touch with him.

On her day off, I call her

Hannah Hi, Greg

Greg 'You're talking to Dad' I ask

Hannah Oh, yeah. I – Mom told you?

Greg 'She did.'

Hannah Yeah, I'm sorry. I didn't know how to tell you. But, yeah, he's been calling, and I picked up

Greg 'He's been calling me, too' I say.

Hannah I know. I think you should talk to him

Greg 'No, I shouldn't' I say

Hannah No, I –

I get where you're coming from, but, Greg. It's been years. We only have one dad

Greg 'What is this' I ask

Hannah I – I just. I don't know. I don't want to – I just think you should talk to him, I don't know

Greg 'He's

He's a terrible man, he *destroyed* our lives'

Hannah He's trying to be better

Greg 'He's homophobic'

Hannah (*taken aback*) He is?

Greg 'He. He's . . . well. I don't know. The last conversation we had, he was. There was this undertone of just. It was like I came home and he was so let down by who his son is. I don't know, Han. He makes me uncomfortable. I don't want to be uncomfortable.'

Hannah Oh.

I understand

Greg You do?

Hannah Yeah, sort of. Listen, he was shit. He did shit. He fucked us over. He fucked so many people over. But, how long can we be mad, you know?

You've got your stuff, I've got mine. I'm not going to tell you what to do, but

I'm gonna say something and you're not going to like it

I think you should go to therapy

Greg 'Oh'

Hannah It's not. It doesn't mean you crazy or anything. I just think. I think you deserve to know peace. And I think a therapist could help you find it.

Greg I hate how right she is. I hate it.

I hate that my sister can be caring and insightful and successful and not even be aware that she is all those things

Hannah It's just an idea Greg, you can take it or leave it.

But a lot of people have been doing it. A lot. And it's all on Zoom.

And it's really. It's really helpful

Greg 'Have you been doing it' I ask

Hannah I have

Greg 'Should I go to yours' I ask

Hannah You should not. At all. By any means.

Greg 'Right, right' I say

And we end our conversation and that night I browse all the in network providers available to me. My insurance is somewhere between sucks ass and really fucking sucks ass. Which is to say – American.

A projection of a scrolling ZocDoc page fills the stage.

After hours of searching, I finally find Doctor Deirdre Thompson. She meets all of my *extensive* criteria, she's stunning, takes my insurance, and her name is Doctor Deirdre. I love alliteration.

I look forward to a session of saying *Doctor Deirdre* until she says

Deirdre Deirdre is really fine. It's better that way.

I want to rid you of any notion of formalities. The way I run my practice is that you and I will just have a conversation.

If something illuminating happens in that conversation, then that's fantastic.

But I do not want to set a precedent for you that something *must* happen.

This should be a pressure free situation.

So, with that said

She leans in, a deep, warm, genuine stare.

Why now?

Greg 'Why now . . . what' I ask

Deirdre Here, now. Why therapy in this moment?

Greg 'My sister made me. Well, she *suggested* it.'

Deirdre And why did she suggest it?

Greg 'She – she has this theory. That, basically, I am holding a grudge with my dad. We don't speak to him. Well, *I* don't. She does now, because – I don't know, because she's a traitor.

But, honestly, I think you'll back me up.'

Deirdre Back you up?

Greg 'Take my side'

Deirdre Why don't you? Talk to your dad, that is?

Greg And I say everything.

It's like someone took a knife to the bubble of trauma that had gone untouched inside of me. All it took was one small poke and suddenly I'm spilling my guts to a stranger via Zoom.

Deirdre What would a conversation with your dad look like?

Greg 'How do you mean?' I ask

Deirdre If you were to, let's say hypothetically, you get on the phone with him right now. And he picks up. And the two of you talk. How would that conversation begin?

Greg 'Oh. I just don't see myself calling him' I say

Deirdre In this hypothetical, let's say you do

Greg 'Well, then. I guess, I'd.

I'd say 'Hi'

Deirdre Interesting. That's so interesting.

What's the first question you'd ask him?

Greg 'Did you break my iPod nano in 2007 or was that really the cleaning lady? No. No. I should be serious I guess. I'm getting the idea that I should be serious'

Deirdre Be whatever you want. Let's keep going

Greg 'I'd ask him how he's doing.'

Deirdre What else?

Greg 'I think. I think I'd want to know like. I think I'd want to ask him about basic stuff like . . .

Like what does he have for breakfast most days.

And, like, how does he take his coffee

Does he get bagels a lot, he used to get bagels a lot when we were kids

I remember he'd always get the weirdest – he'd get a cinnamon raisin bagel with salmon cream cheese. And it was so weird.

I think I'd want to know if he still gets that

A Little Treat   29

And I'd want to know where he lives – like, does he live in a house? Or an apartment? Or like, like a condo.

My mom saw where he lives once but I cut her off before she could describe it to me, I think I'd want to know that

And if there's pictures of me and Hannah in his home

And if he has, like, a dog

Or a cat

We grew up with both, but I feel like he didn't like either

But maybe he likes them both now

Or maybe he can't have one because of his job –

A job, I'd want to know what kind of job he has.

Does he have a job?

And is he single? Or is he dating? Or did he like meet one of those women who writes letters to inmates

Is he alone? Is he lonely? Or does he have someone

And if he does have someone, do they know about me?

And do they understand it, do they understand me, why I don't . . .

Or do they think I'm just some fucking. Some asshole.

And does he think that?

Does he hate me?

Or does he get it?

Does he understand it?

Yeah I think.

I think I'd want to know about all of that.

But first I think I'd want to know what he has for breakfast.'

And then Deirdre says

Deirdre I'm so sorry, my Zoom cut out, I, I only caught the last bit

What'd you say, you want to know what he has for breakfast?

Greg That afternoon, after Deirdre and I wrap up our session, I open my window and fresh air pours in.

The session makes me feel oddly free. So I go outside and begin to walk down the avenue.

It's so desolate, I take off my phallic mask, put into my pocket and breathe in deep.

I walk for nearly two hours, from 205th street down to 115th.

A projection of the night sky fills the stage, warm and summery. New York at its peak.

I've never seen anything like

Or heard anything like it.

The city is completely silent. For maybe the first time in its history.

And I pull open my phone. And consider breaking the silence with one of my dad's voicemails.

Since we haven't spoken, my dad has left what I can only assume is at least 100 voicemails for me.

They vary in length, sometimes they're four seconds long, sometimes they go to almost two minutes.

I have never listened to a single one.

Because inside each one is my father, bitter, and angry, spitting fire, ready to confront me – about my life, my choices, who I am. All of it.

For a moment, I feel equipped to handle it. And my hand hovers over the play button.

The alarm rings.

But suddenly it's 7 p.m.

And I think silence feels like the perfect treat for the night. So I put my phone away and walk home.

As each week passes, I begin to look forward to my sessions with Deirdre.

My dad continues to call. And the calls continue to go to voicemail.

And as the virus rages on, my fear only increases. I start to only go out at night.

Samuel grows concerned.

Samuel What about joining my poker nights, Greg. It's cute, it's fun.

Greg One night, I say yes. Then, he tells me it starts at 7. I decide my treat for that night will be the joy of my own company and skip out.

Besides, resources for treats are starting to dwindle.

The night before I skip poker night, my treat was supposed to be a pint of Jeni's ice cream. Without warning, my Instacart shopper replaced it with Breyers. The two aren't comparable, any fool can see that.

The night before that, I burnt the lasagna that I had clung that day's hopes and dreams to.

I begin to exhaust every piece of media available for consumption. Did you know there's a Real Housewives of Australia? I couldn't understand a word they said.

A month passes and my treats go odd places.

I find myself on Grindr, sexting with a Republican who has a micropenis.

One night, I *sob* over how good a microwave mug cake is.

I don't mean a small cry – I mean *deep, heaving sobs* over this cake.

The treats vacillate in quality and quantity and I'm having a hard time coping with this

I decide it's time to finally tell Deirdre about this.

After explaining it in its full detail during our Thursday session, her face makes a small twist then deflates into this stare that just . . . sits in the room. She moves enough to make it clear her Zoom hasn't gone out, but I am wondering if she's having stomach trouble

'Deirdre' I ask

Deirdre Yeah, no, I'm here. I'm just . . . I don't know what to say

Greg 'How do you mean' I ask

Deirdre You have a remarkable ability to . . . to build your own world.

Greg 'Are you judging me?'

Deirdre No – I?

Greg 'Is this about last week? Because I felt like you were weird last week, after our conversation'

Deirdre Well, in a way yes. I do think it's odd you had no idea what the protests are about

Greg 'It's not that I didn't know, I just didn't know about them until last week'

Deirdre (*a small ire fills her voice, like it has been siting there, waiting to poke out*) Greg, last week was June 25th. The Black Lives Matter movement started in the beginning of June

Greg 'Right, and since, since you told me about it, I posted a black square. I signed petitions, I donated to a bunch of causes, I even Venmo'd this one place, I even, I even stopped watching the Bon Appetit Test Kitchen.

Deirdre (*with a clip*)   Greg, that's great, but –

Greg   '. . . but what' I ask

Deirdre (*controlling herself*)   Let's drop this

Greg   'No, I feel like you're calling me racist'

Deirdre (*all of her boundaries rapidly disappearing*)   I didn't call you racist. Greg. But if that's your only concern, then you've completely missed the point.

Somewhat embarrassed.

I'm sorry. That was. That was unprofessional of me. That. I.

Greg, last week threw me. In a way I did not anticipate. You know, I'm a person too. I'm watching everything happening in the world right now and to hear you – And part of – part of my job as your provider is to know when I can't be your provider

Greg   'You're breaking up with me?'

Deirdre   No. I. Well.

No, I. I just can't be your provider any more, that's all. I. I'm sorry Greg, I really am. I just, for whatever reason, this, this isn't working for me. And for you, in turn. I'm going, I'm sending you a list of providers who will give you wonderful care. Fantastic care. And I'm not going to charge you for the last two sessions. I. I think we should end this here.

Greg   And she hangs up. And my head is spinning. And my alarm goes off and I see the time. And I start to compile a list of possible treats for the evening

Greg's *phone is heard ringing.*

Then my phone rings. And I decide that I will indulge in silence, so I ignore it.

Until it rings again. And I decide I still deserve that silence.

And then it rings again, and I see it's my mom, who never calls three times in a row.

Something about commanding attention, not demanding it

Ellen Greg?

Greg 'Hi, Ma' I say

Ellen Hi, honey

Greg I can hear the concern in her voice

'What's happening'

Ellen Well, honey . . .

Greg 'What, Ma, what's going on?'

Ellen It's your father. He, um. He's in the hospital. He, he got it.

Greg 'Got it?'

Ellen He has the, the – he's, uh, he's in the hospital. I guess he had it for almost a week and then, uh, they, they had to intubate him

Greg 'What does that mean?'

Ellen He's not doing well, Greg. He's probably –

Well. He's. He's not breathing on his own.

Greg 'So, you're saying'

Ellen It's Hannah's hospital. It's how we found out, apparently he's been in there for a few days. But no one knew, no one was contacted. And she saw his name today and so she, she went to see him on her rotation and.

She said it's. Well, sweetheart, she said it's only a matter of time.

Greg 'Oh.' I say

Ellen I think. Hannah might be able to get you on FaceTime with him.

Greg 'What do you mean?'

Ellen So you could talk to him before, before he. Before he goes.

Greg 'I don't. I don't –'

Ellen I know you don't talk to him sweetheart, but you should. The man's. Honey.

You should say goodbye to him

Greg 'Ma, what am I saying goodbye to? Wouldn't I have to say hello first?'

Ellen Honey, I know you're steadfast in your conviction. But. But he is your father. And he's. This is your last chance.

Please, just. *For me*, just so I know. Just so he can go and I can have a clear conscience that both of my kids had closure.

Just, FaceTime Hannah and she'll go down to his room and. You can say whatever you want to him.

He probably won't be able to even talk to you, but just.

Please, for my sake.

Please

Greg My mom and I hang up. And I consider my treat for the day being a nap. Ignoring what she said. Not calling Hannah. Not seeing my dad. Letting the chapter just close on its own.

Then Hannah FaceTimes me.

I answer without realizing my fingers are swiping open the call

Hannah looks tired, her forehead marked with the impression of a face-shield

Hannah Hi Greggy

Greg 'Hi' I say, 'what's happening?'

Hannah I'm hanging in there. You know.

Mom said you were going to call me but I knew you wouldn't so I figured I'd call you

I'm gonna take you down to him now, okay?

Greg *sits in stunned silence after* **Hannah** *says this, processing.*

Hannah *breaks it.*

Hannah Greg?

Greg 'Yeah, sorry. Yeah'

Hannah Okay, I'm starting down

A projection fills the stage, an abstract blurred view of an overcrowded hospital.

The noise of that hospital plays softly as **Greg** *speaks.*

Greg Hannah suits up in a white cloak, face mask, face shield, and gloves. Honestly it's kind of chic if you forget the circumstances. She looks like a gorgeous sewage worker.

She begins to walk down the hallway, struggling to hold the phone straight in her gloved hands.

But I see the blurry background of the overstuffed hospital.

Beds in every corner of the hallway, overstuffed rooms.

Exhausted, exasperated staff.

We make it down to the lower level.

Hannah continues to walk across this floor, just as overstuffed with staff just as tired, until she makes it to a bed in a corner room, next to a window.

A small, emaciated outline of a man lays beneath blankets and tubes.

A Little Treat 37

And I recognize that this is what my father looks like

The top of his head is decorated with a large tuft of salt and pepper gray hair

A beard puffs out from under the oxygen mask and I begin to consider what he might look like free of all the tubes and machinery.

If it's what I think, then it's not a good look. My dad's face is far too oblong for a beard

Hannah Dad?

Greg I hear Hannah say, as if that's natural.

Hannah Dad? Can you hear me

The projection shifts to show an abstracted view of **Lou***'s hospital room.*

Greg And I see his fragile frame move under the blankets

Hannah Hi Dad. I have someone on the phone who wants to talk to you.

It's Greg

Greg And the movement increases, his head moves. And Hannah moves the phone closer. The only thing I can see behind the beard and the mask are his bright blue eyes, with bags puffing out beneath them

And I hear Hannah say

Hannah Dad, do you see Greg? It's Greggy.

Greg And I hear someone say something to Hannah and she says

Hannah Greg, I have to go run to handle something, but I'll be right back. I'm going to prop the phone up, why don't you chat with Dad

Greg And she leaves. And we sit there.

And I think about all the things I could say. I think about telling him about my life. Telling him what he's missed. Telling him what I've missed.

I think about telling him I forgive him.

I think about ending it with a clean slate

I think about saying all that I can fit into all the time that we have together

But instead.

The sound of the hospital grows louder, with the sound of a heart monitor and ventilator reverberates.

Greg *sits there, struggling to find words. A long, extended beat is filled by the sounds of the machines growing louder and louder as* **Greg** *stares into his father's eyes and experiences what must be all seven stages of grief.*

I say nothing.

Hannah comes back into the room and picks the phone up, asks if I need more time and I shake my head no.

She ends the call.

That night, he dies.

The projection of the hospital fades away.

That day also marks the first day in over five years that I go without a little treat.

Early the next morning I am sitting outside of my building, when Sam walks by, and sits down next to me, bags in his hand.

'You're up early' I say

Samuel   I was throwing my TV away

Greg   I look at the curb, and sure enough, his TV is sitting next to the trash, the screen shattered, glass everywhere.

'What happened to it' I ask

Samuel I threw a mug at it

Greg 'Oh' I say

Samuel I got mad at the fucking news.

Greg 'Right' I say

Samuel They had some fucker on, some kid, a few years older than you, probably, some infectious disease specialist, and he goes, he says 'Well, what we're enduring right now is nearly identical to the AIDS epidemic, both, uh, pathologically,' he says, 'and politically' then goes one with some statement and I just about lost it and, there you go

Greg 'You broke your TV' I say

Samuel I broke my TV

Greg And he sits up straight and goes

Samuel It's just such a ridiculous argument, I mean, anyone. Anyone who lived through that. Please. Anyone who *lived* through that. Everyday it was like waking up and your neighbor's apartment was on fire and you were calling the fire department and they were saying 'Best of luck to you' –

Fuck, they weren't even saying best of luck, they didn't even answer the phone.

Greg 'Right' I say. 'I'd break my TV too'

Samuel I spoke to your mom

Greg He says. 'You did' I say?

Samuel We exchanged numbers last month. Just so she has eyes on the ground.

She told me.

Greg 'Right' I say

Samuel I remember everything you told me about him, though

Greg 'You do' I say. I'm shocked, mostly because I hardly remember a thing Sam tells me.

Samuel Of course I do. Listen.

People are. Well people fucking suck. They do. People can be terrible. Awful. So. So cruel. In ways you can't even fathom. Even when you think you've reached the limits of someone's cruelty, you haven't.

But the thing is. People can be so, so, so. Well I don't even know if there's a word for how wonderful people can be.

It's a terrifying thing to know – that so much pain can exist in a world as beautiful as ours.

Greg And then he hands me a bag and says

Samuel I got you bagels. Make yourself breakfast. And call me the second you need me. And not a second later.

Greg And he gets up.

Later, when I get inside, I look in the bag and see there's salmon cream cheese. And a cinnamon raisin bagel. And I do it, I make my dad's order. And it smells like Sunday mornings when I'm six and I'm looking up at him at the register in the deli ordering his breakfast.

And I bite into it.

And I vomit. All over my couch.

And right after, my mom calls me

Ellen What do you know about Zoom?

Greg 'What?' I ask

Ellen What do you know about Zoom? We have to host your father's memorial

Greg '*We* have to?' I ask

Ellen Well, who do you think is going to do it?

Greg 'I'm kind of in the middle of something'

Ellen What could you be busy with right now?

Greg 'There's vomit everywhere'

Ellen Vomit? Vomit? Do you have stomach flu

Greg 'No, I – nothing. I. I know how to work Zoom'

Ellen Okay, good. Also figure out what you're going to say

Greg 'What I'm going to say?' I ask

Ellen You're going to have to eulogize him

Greg 'You're kidding me'

Ellen Hannah hates public speaking. And you don't, so it's going to have to be you

Greg 'I'm not speaking, Mom'

Ellen What if I write the eulogy? If I write it, will you read it? Honey, I know this isn't ideal. And I'm sorry to ask it of you, but I think. Not just for you, for me, for Hannah. It would feel really nice if we. If we closed out your father's life in a nice, in a peaceful way. It would mean a lot to us.

Greg And I look at the puddle of puke on my couch and assess the situation and my willingness to argue and I just say 'fine'

Ellen (*billowing with relief*)   Oh thank god

Greg With Deidre out of the picture, I have no one to sort through this with. So I sit on my thoughts until 7 p.m. rolls around and I've run out of options. Unemployment spent another week forgetting to pay me so I ordered just bare necessities in groceries. I had to cancel Hulu and Netflix for the month, I have nothing to watch.

And I open Grindr. It's not that I'm horny or that I'm planning on meeting up with anyone. I'm just – it would be nice to feel wanted right now.

And I begin messaging people

No one responds

Until finally

A Grindr notification is heard. The message projects onto the stage, from a profile with a headless torso as its profile picture.

Hey Cutie, he says. He thinks I'm cute.

We begin to message each other. And the conversation is going shockingly well.

Messages fill the stage, sweet, polite, and charming on both ends.

His name is Derrick. He's twenty-seven. He is a software engineer who lives on the Upper East Side. He misses his family, but they're from Canada. He can't get back home. *The pandemic's been tough* he tells me. *No shit* I think. We text for almost an hour. Sweet messages back and forth. He tells me all about his life in the city. How he loves it but sometimes he's scared by it.

I tell him I feel the same way. How it's the only place I've ever wanted to be but some days it feels like the last place I should be. But some days it feels like it's completely mine.

Right! he says. *Exactly!*

Then he asks me to go over to his apartment.

'I'm not going out' I say. *Why* he says. 'Pandemic haha' I say. *Really?* he says. 'Really haha' I say. 'Haha'.

And he says nothing.

He blocks me.

And I look up from my phone. And the room is still empty.

The stage becomes filled with abstract Zoom boxes of all the attendees of Lou's funeral.

Greg *sits in the center.*

It takes nearly two hours to teach my Uncle Mo and Aunt Claire how to install Zoom.

A minister from my dad's church leads the service.

I am shocked to discover my dad went to church, let alone had a minister who knew him well.

Before it's my turn to speak, the Minister says

Minister We're all flawed. We all make mistakes. Lou was no different. He was a man. Who spent the latter half of his life trying to right his wrongs.

When all is said and done, Lou lived a meaningful life. He was a friend to all, an essential member in Fairfield County, and most importantly, a dedicated father. He loved his children. Not one conversation went by where he didn't mention his daughter Hannah, and his son, Gregory. And I am sure he is looking down right now, beaming with pride at the two people they are today. And I believe we have some remarks from his son, Gregory.

Greg I can feel everyone's eyes turn to my little box on Zoom.

I look down at my computer and begin to read the eulogy my mom wrote

He clears his throat.

'Thank you all for being here

He clears it again.

For being here today.

He clears his throat.

Excuse me.

44 A Little Treat

Um'

He clears his throat again.

Then I hear my Uncle Mo say

Uncle Mo Greg, do you need some water?

Greg 'No, I'm good Uncle Mo. Thanks

Uh.

Um.

Um.'

And I look away from the eulogy and say

'Yeah, I just want to thank you all for being here. And. Yeah, just uh. Thanks. I know Zoom is annoying, so. So. Yeah. Thanks.'

And I sit back

And the Minister asks me

Minister Is that it?

Greg And I say 'that's it'

And I see my mom's face drop.

The Zoom boxes fade away.

Greg's *phone rings.*

Within minutes after the memorial, my mom calls

Ellen What the fuck was that

Greg 'What do you mean, Mom' I ask

Ellen Don't – *don't*. Why didn't you read what I wrote?

Greg 'I couldn't do it'

Ellen You couldn't do it or you didn't want to do it?

Greg 'I couldn't'

Ellen Bullshit. I went on one of your tours, you spewed out an entire script while biking and singing. You could've done whatever you wanted

Greg 'Then, fine, Ma' I say, 'I didn't want to.'

Ellen That's selfish, Greg. You had the choice to close the chapter in a nice way and you chose not to

Greg 'I had no interest in being there, let alone speaking. You tried to get me to lie about who this man was to me'

Ellen It really, without fail, it always goes back to you. Doesn't it?

Greg 'What's that supposed to mean?'

Ellen It means exactly what it is supposed to mean – I needed you to read that eulogy. Hannah needed it. We all needed it. And I told you as much

I begged you, I *begged you*. I said 'Please, please just say it – for me'

You ignored it because the only thing that mattered were your feelings about him.

Well guess what Greg, you're not the only one who lived this experience.

We all lived the same experiences you lived, with the same man.

You think it was all exclusive to you.

It was not.

We just wanted it to end. We just wanted a decade of this fraught, this, this – all the pain, just to close out in some meaningful way. For it to all finally have *some* meaning. You robbed us of that. You said you'd do it and you didn't.

Greg 'You could've done it yourself, if it was so important' I say

Ellen When was the last time I asked you for a favor?

Greg I say nothing and she says

Ellen When was the last time I asked you to do something for me. I cannot remember a time in years, *years* where I have asked anything of you, other than to call me and to come home for the holidays.

Christ, Gregory. You couldn't muster up more than fifteen seconds of bullshit to just appease us.

To take care of us.

I've spent so much time taking care of you. I've always thought at some point, maybe, you'd consider returning the favor.

But you're . . . you're . . .

Greg 'What?' I say, 'I'm what? Say what you're gonna say'

Ellen I wish I experienced this whole pandemic thing through your eyes. I do.

I wish I spent it indulging myself, sequestering myself, treating myself.

I wish I knew how to do that.

Instead of drowning myself in this puddle of concern every night for a son who doesn't even call me.

And when you do, when you do call me, which only happens because I have begged you to pick up the phone, all you do is talk about what that night's treat is. What you'll be doing for yourself.

But you know what I realized, today. You know what I realized.

I don't think I know what it sounds like for you to ask me how I'm doing.

I don't think I've heard you ever say 'How are you?'

Maybe asking you to read the eulogy was too much, I don't know. Maybe it wasn't fair. I should've let you get through this how you get through it, I guess. I don't know. I should've had the minister read something.

I don't know. I'm. I'm sorry.

Maybe I'm wrong there, but I think I'm pretty right about everything else

Greg 'What does that mean?' I ask

Ellen Ask me how I'm doing, Greg

Greg 'Mom' I say

Ellen Not great.

Melting with exhaustion, pain, hurt, frustration, a million things.

I'm not doing too great.

Greg And she hangs up.

An hour later, it's 7 p.m.

I have no money.

I have no groceries.

I have no Real Housewives.

I have no treat.

And I need to be anywhere but my apartment.

I take the eggplant mask Samuel made me and one of the medical grade ones my mom dropped off.

I double mask and walk out of my building.

As I walk, the glow of sunset fills the sky

New York City at sunset fills the stage, moving and abstracted, gorgeous and glowing. The sound of a semi-active city fills the stage.

48 A Little Treat

The streets are busier than they've been. Filled with people gathering, eating out, laughing. Pretending like life is normal. Pretending like any of this is normal.

I speed down Broadway.

The stage transitions from New York City at sunset to New York City at night.

By 8:15 the sun has set and I am on 103rd Street. I continue walking down Broadway.

The Upper West Side is packed. And I see a restaurant filled with people dining outside

And the waiters are decked out in essentially hazmat gear

I become incensed. It is the first moment in the evening when I feel a sincere disconnect from my body and my brain

The first moment in this night where the two are not working in tandem with each other

My body indulges my gut while my brain begs it not to

And I scream at a family as I wait to cross the street

I yell to them

'GO HOME'

And the man at the table says

Man What?

Greg And I say 'WHAT IS WRONG WITH YOU, GO HOME'

And he says

Man Mind your own fucking business, pal

Greg And I shout 'THOUSANDS OF PEOPLE ARE DEAD BUT THANK GOD YOU WERE ABLE TO ORDER A BASKET OF STEAK FRIES'

And then he says

Man THEY'RE ONION RINGS, JERK OFF

Greg And then the man leans forward, tells his son it's okay, and he wipes his kid's mouth. And suddenly, the oddest warmth fills me. And I want to call my dad.

I turn a corner and open my phone and pull up my voicemail.

My thumb hovers over the play button and I consider all the vitriol sitting there, waiting for me. The flames of anger that mark the last things my father left me before leaving this earth.

I consider all the ways he'll tell me what an awful person I am.

How I've abandoned him, misunderstood him, devalued him. Hurt him.

I toy with everything he could possibly say and then

I hit play.

Lou Hey Greggy, it's dad.

I, uh. I was talking to Hannah and she said that you, uh, that you might be interested in talking to me again or something.

And I don't know if that's true or if she was just blowin' smoke, but, well.

It made me really happy to hear.

And, uh. I just miss you kid, I miss you a lot.

And I'm really sorry. I really am.

Han showed me this video from Christmas last year and you look good, kid. You look really good. And you sound good, too.

I think about some of the shit I said, Greg, when I got out. I was a prick. I probably still am a prick, who knows.

But, kid, you, you and Hannah. You're everything. My everything. I'm so proud of you, Greggy. Of who you are. Of. Of everything.

Listen, I don't blame you if you don't want to talk to me. But if you get this and think about calling. I go to bed every night with my ringer on, just in case you call.

Every night.

No matter the time, I'll pick up.

I promise.

I love you.

Okay, uh, buhbye.

Greg I stand.

I put my phone in my pocket.

I keep walking.

I walk so fast, I tear through lights, a cab honks at me. I keep walking.

I keep walking and the buildings feel so tall, it feels like the whole city is going to swallow me whole.

And all I want to do is hover above it.

And that's when I realize where I am

On the corner of Broadway and 44th.

A few years ago, I temped in this building for about two months.

They never locked the roof access door and we'd go up on there on Fridays and have drinks together.

Me and these people who wanted to be my friends.

They were so nice.

And they tried *so* hard.

A Little Treat 51

They'd invite me out, they'd invite me to dinner, they'd invite me to parties,

And it wasn't –

I *wanted* to be their friends. I wanted to *be* at their parties.

They'd invite me to the roof.

They'd invite me, every Friday, for two months straight, up to the roof. And we'd go up and they'd pour drinks but I couldn't do it, I couldn't stay. I'd leave before 7.

I don't even remember their names.

In fact, the only thing I remember is that the roof access door is left unlocked.

And that they never took my key card back.

And I go through the part of my wallet that is all old gift cards and I find the keycard.

And I press it up to the door

And I can feel the small part of my body hoping that it'll be rejected. That the door will stay locked and I'll keep walking. I can feel that small part of my body tick

But the door unlocks

And I feel my legs move forward, into the building.

Projection shifts from the city at night to the interior of the building.

To the elevator

The projection then transitions to the elevator, climbing up floors.

Up to the fifty-second floor

Up to the roof access door

I go to push it, it is still unlocked

I walk out onto the roof

52 A Little Treat

The projection shifts to the top of the New York City skyline at night, gorgeous, intimidating, insurmountable.

A light breeze fills the stage from both stage left and stage right.

I look out at the city

This city

This beautiful, terrifying, unforgiving, endlessly demanding

Perfect city

I want it to be mine. All I've ever wanted is for it to be mine.

And I feel the small part of my body pulling back

But I feel the rest of my body pull a chair up to the barrier of the roof

He begins to rise onto the stool, to stand atop it.

And use it to climb onto the ledge

He rises full on the stool and stands up straight.

And stand on top of it

Right on top of it

Towering over the rest of the city

At eye level with the peak of the other skyscrapers

And I look out

And I think

How stupid was I to think that this city belongs to me

Is everything

Does everything have to feel so

So impermanent

And I started to assess all the things in my life I've denied myself

All the big joys I've passed over in trade of simple pleasures

Because I hate the feeling of being overwhelmed

And now all I am is overwhelmed
And now all I am is alone
And now all I am is scared
Holy shit, I'm scared. I am, I'm so fucking scared. But the thing is, the thing is, it's such a familiar feeling
Like, I've known this feeling my whole life
And I begin to recognize that this is my resting state.

This is who I am.

I refused to eat what would fill me

For fear it would make me sick.

And now I'm starving

And I look out and –

Oh Christ

If I take one step, it goes

I go from

I go from here

To there

A deep terror enters his voice.

If I just take one step there I go

I go

I go

I would

I would JUST

Projection of the entirety of buildings begins to sweep up the entire stage, at the speed of someone falling down them. Rapid and vast.

54   A Little Treat

The fans fill the stage with wind.

The clap of thunder is heard.

It begins to rain.

No, no, no, no

No, you have to understand

I don't want to

I want to just

Fuck I want a treat

A real one. A real treat. A big, huge, fucking treat.

I want a moment

The buildings begin to slow down, while the rain continues to fall.

A moment of joy that isn't manufactured

And instead I'm standing here, on the edge of a building, surveying the world.

How did I get here. How did we get here. All it took was one tragedy.

To give way to all the other tragedy

And to collapse.

But I'm standing here

And I'm so alone

I'm so alone

Last night I thought about texting my twink manager just to say hi

I'm so alone.

And, and, you know that was never the plan but it just sorta happened because I got.

I got scared

(*Softly.*) I just got scared

Of all of it, of the – of existence

But I think I love existence

I know I love existence

I know I want –

I want the before to be different and I don't know what the after looks like

Thunder claps, the storm becomes louder.

And it begins to rain, it begins to pour

I take a moment and survey just how precarious my position is

How one wrong step will end it all

And how now the surface is getting slippery

And I'm not sure how I'll get down

But I need to get down

I need to

I don't just want to

I need to

And I tell myself

I tell myself

Take a moment

Calm down

Don't even consider falling

Just imagine

Imagine *everything* is *safe*

He closes his eyes.

Imagine everything is calm

The thunder claps.

Imagine the thunder is music

A soft hum plays.

Imagine the rain is confetti

Confetti begins to softly fall on the stage.

And you are at a party.

You stay at the party.

You love being at the party.

The stone you're standing on, it's just grass

And the noise of the traffic below you, it's all your friends

It's all the people who

Laughing

And talking

And celebrating

We are all together

Everything is fine

You just have to get off the ledge

He opens his eyes, gently, precariously, fearfully, but calmly lowers himself back down onto the stool and sits up.

The projection fades, so does the music, and the confetti stops falling.

That night I walk home.

I don't sleep.

That morning, I find my new therapist.
The one with the pantsuits. She's fabulous, I love her.

The days have gone on. So have I.

You know, none of it has ever made sense.

None of it

You like to think that out of the ashes comes something better but.

In a lot of ways, the world feels worse for wear.

In ways you can't even imagine

Sometimes doesn't it –

Doesn't it feel like it'll swallow you whole?

But sometimes.

Sometimes

I wake up

He fills with a twinkle, melting with joy, brimming with hope, marinating in what things have become.

I wake up

And the sun is shining

And it's bouncing off the trees

And hitting all the buildings

And the city is brimming with life

Across the street, kids play in the park

While their parents watch

And birds chirp

And I step outside

And begin to move down the blocks

Five blocks down, at the church, a couple is getting married

And bells are tolling

And people are cheering

And I keep walking

I keep walking

And at the tip of Central Park

These friends are looking for a spot to have a picnic

But the ground is soaking wet

They don't care, they decide

They set their things down

And say *this is good*

And I keep walking

I make it to Midtown, where a line of tourists are waiting outside for a matinee of The Lion King

This boy looks at his mom

And he asks if the show is long

And she looks back at him

And she says

'It's just long enough'

And I keep walking

I walk Downtown

Make my way through Soho

People are just getting out of work

This guy looks nervous, I think he has a date

He's fixing his shirt when he drops his phone

I hand it to him

I keep walking

I walk

and I make my way through FiDi

And I thank god I don't work in finance

And I keep walking

And I realize I've never been on the Ferry

I've lived in this city for almost a decade now and I've never been on the Ferry

And I walk

I walk over

I get a ticket

I step onto the Ferry

Over to the tip of the boat

Among all the people going home for the day

The city gets smaller in the distance

And the sun begins to set

But before it does

It gets brighter

And brighter

And brighter

And I look up

And the warmth of the rays spill all over me

The stage becomes filled with warmth, pouring out everywhere.

He basks in it, overcome by survival, overcome by existence.

And it feels

So warm

It feels

He is percolating with joy, stirring in it, it's almost too much.

Almost.

It feels like

I feels like –

Like –

Like –

I –

As everything inside of him pours out, something tickles his nose.

I –

I –

One second –

I'm sorry

His nose wrinkles.

I'm gonna

He smiles. He knows.

I'm gonna sneeze

He does.

Blackout.

End of Play.

Discover. Read. Listen. Watch.

A NEW WAY TO ENGAGE WITH PLAYS

This award-winning digital library features over 3,000 playtexts, 400 audio plays, 300 hours of video and 360 scholarly books.

Playtexts published by Methuen Drama, The Arden Shakespeare, Faber & Faber, Playwrights Canada Press, Aurora Metro Books and Nick Hern Books.

Audio Plays from L.A. Theatre Works featuring classic and modern works from the oeuvres of leading American playwrights.

Video collections including films of live performances from the RSC, The Globe and The National Theatre, as well as acting masterclasses and BBC feature films and documentaries.

FIND OUT MORE:
www.dramaonlinelibrary.com • @dramaonlinelib

For a complete listing of
Methuen Drama titles, visit:
www.bloomsbury.com/drama

Follow us on X and keep up to date with
our news and publications
@MethuenDrama